ADVERTISING
SPOT ILLUSTRATIONS
of the Twenties and Thirties

1,593 Cuts

Edited by LESLIE CABARGA

Dover Publications, Inc., New York

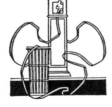

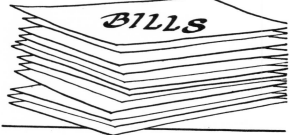

HERE'S

MONEY

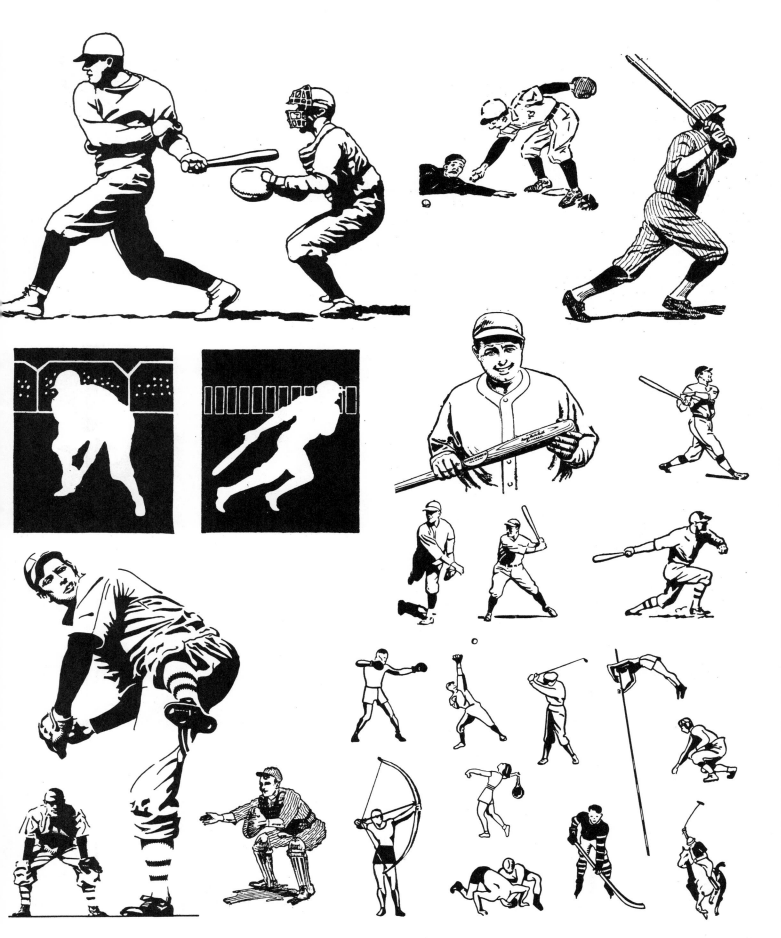

FOOTBALL

Tee

Tee-Totalers

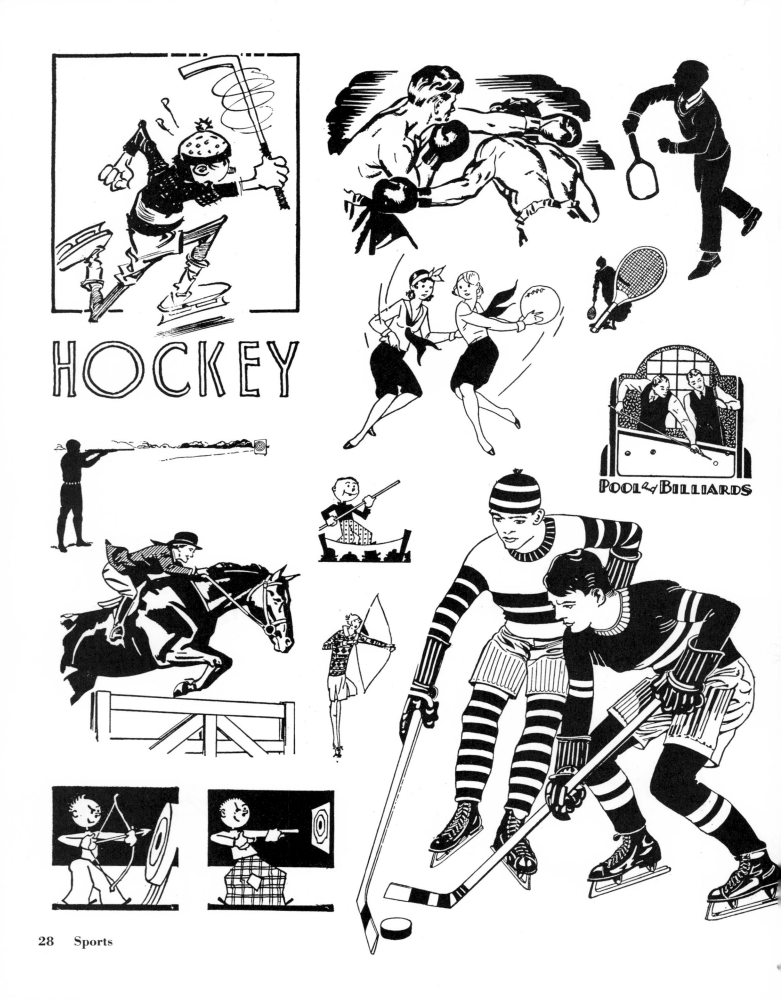

HOCKEY

POOL and BILLIARDS

TOUCHE!

Move?

Fishing

Pour le Sport

Skating

FUNERAL SERVICE

COAL and COKE

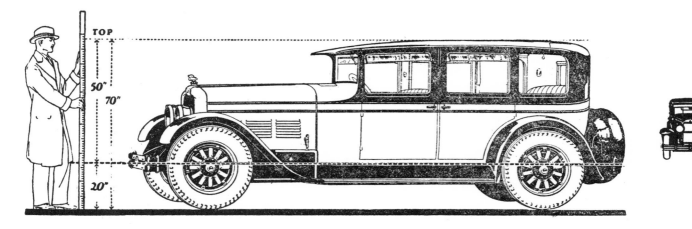

SERVICE
COAL
More Heat Less Waste

RADIATORS

BATTERY
SERVICE

LearnAutos

Need help?

Windshields

replaced

TWICE
Daily

Garage

MOTOR REPAIR

Let us tell you WHAT'S WRONG

WRECKING SERVICE

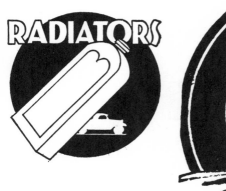
RADIATORS

SERVICE

Let us tell you WHAT'S WRONG

NO PITCHING !

NO SIDE-SWAY !   NO ROLL !

AUTOMOBILE SERVICE

VALVE GRINDING

GAS

full measure:

IGNITION SERVICE

Get-Away!

Repairs

We grease to please

YOU'LL BE SATISFIED

BATTERIES

Valves ground

Garage

BIG VALUES in **Used car's**

Dependable
Taxi service

RADIATORS

Auto Laundry

Auto Glass

Let us doctor
your radiator

Accidents
WILL HAPPEN

Let us fix 'em

Used Cars

Parking

DAY and NITE
pull·in
service

PHONE US

Auto Glass

Auto Insurance

Ignition Service

Motor Repair

Dependable
Taxi service

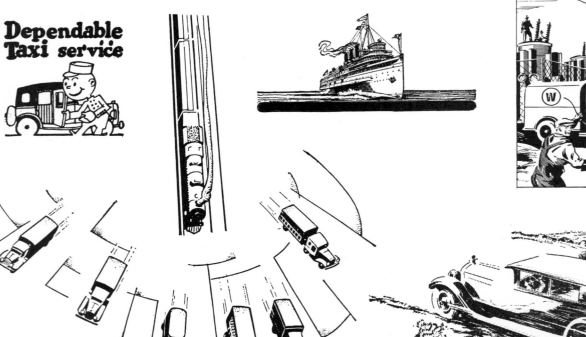

The Season for Travel is Close at Hand~~

Smart and Homelike

TRAVEL by BUS

Approved
MOTEL
TOURIST
HOME

The Place to STOP When You GO

PRETTY SWANK

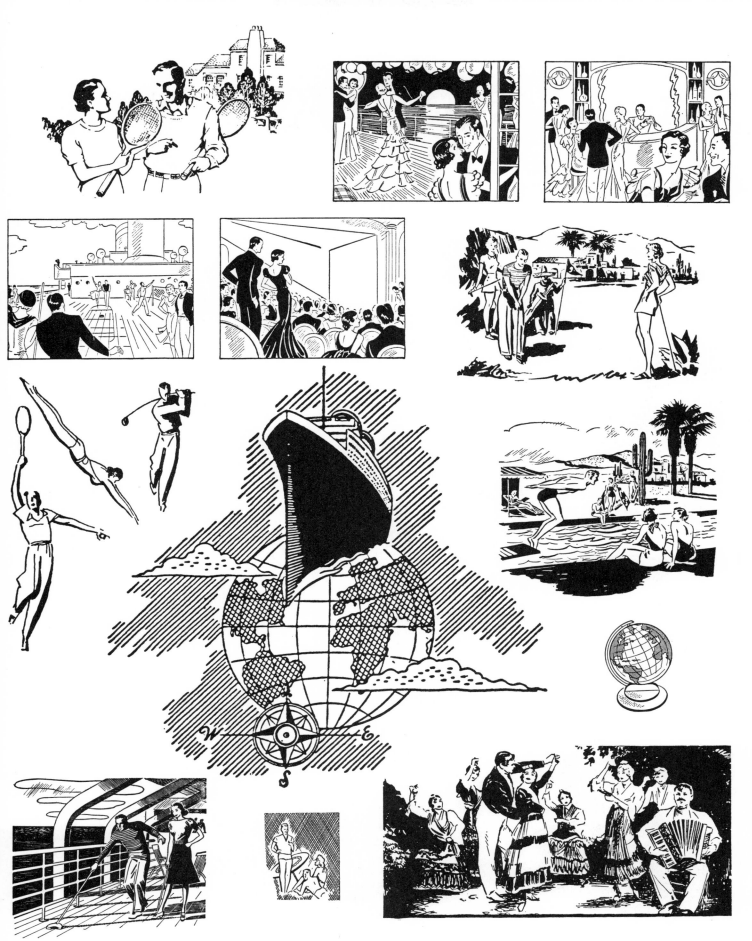

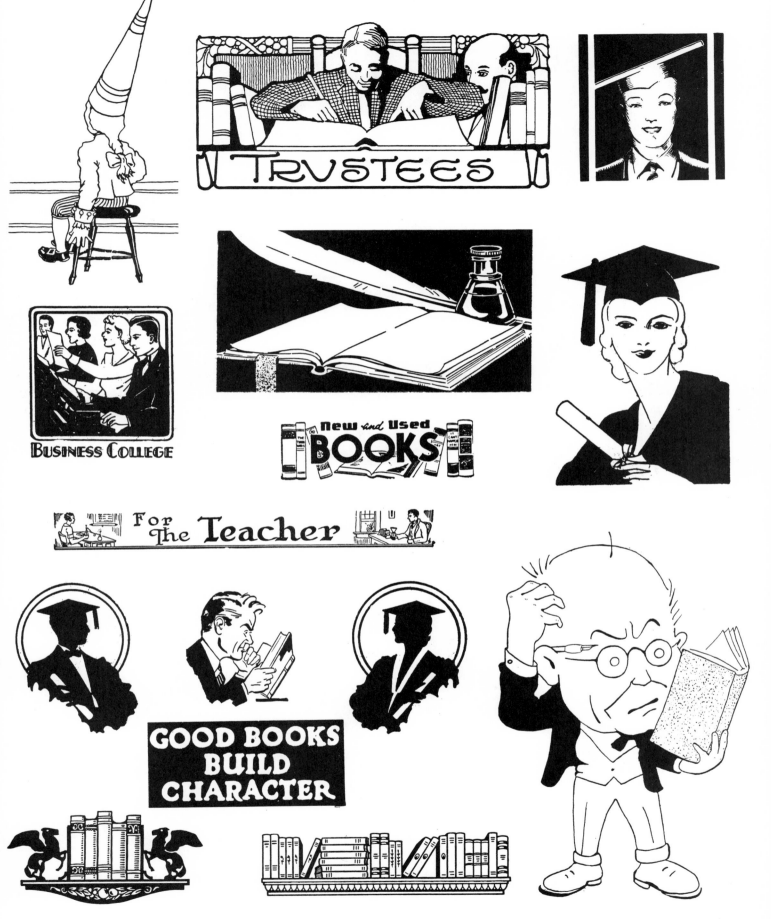

TRUSTEES

BUSINESS COLLEGE

New and Used BOOKS

For The Teacher

GOOD BOOKS BUILD CHARACTER

Books and
more Books

WHO PAYS *YOUR* Hospital Bills?

Will *YOUR* Wife Come to *This?*

Stop That Pain!

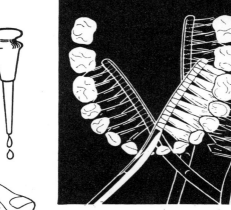

Troubled by Headaches?

UPPER

8 7 6 5 4 3 2 1 1 2 3 4 5 6 7 8

LOWER

DENTISTRY

RUPTURE

UPPER

PATIENT'S RIGHT   PATIENT'S LEFT

LOWER

"A Swell Affair"

BACK TO NATURE!

WALL EXERCISER

HAND GRIPS

SKIP ROPE

FOOT STRAP

We make Keys

Mechanic and Broker

KEYS

MACHINE SHOP

Ver'min Exterminator

Weather Stripping

Carpenter and repair work

Carpenter and repair work

CARPENTRY
ALL KINDS OF
BUILDING

Asbestos Covering

CONTRACTORS

House wrecking

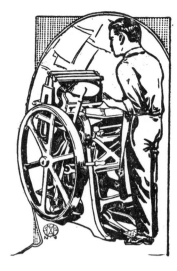

ADDING MACHINES

Job PRINT SHOP

Commercial

Photography

Photo Finishing

ART-DEPARTMENT

Distinctive Gifts

ART and GIFT SHOP

Be an Artist

Earn $75 to $100 a week in ART

Check in

PAINTS

HOUSE PAINT
ANY COLOR

PAINTING

PAINT

House Painting

House Painting

PAINTERS

PAINT UP!

EXPERT Piano moving

Packing Household goods

Transfer
LOCAL and LONG DISTANCE

LUMBER & BUILDING MATERIALS

LUMBER

BUILDER of HOMES

LUMBER
MILLWORK

Better LUMBER for Better Homes

LUMBER

LUMBER
FOR THAT NEW HOME!
CALL US FOR AN ESTIMATE

Fireproof Storage

Plastering

ANY SIZE JOB

PLASTERING

IPLAJTIERIINGr

PLASTIC WORK

WALL PAPER

Beautiful designs

PLASTERING

Shades

BOXES
WE MAKE ANY
SHAPE OR FORM

STORM
WINDOWS

SCREENS

PLASTERING

UPHOLSTERING

WALLPAPER

AWNINGS

AWNINGS

Window
Cleaning

Service

Window Cleaning Service

WINDOW CLEANING

Window Trimmer's

STORE SIGNS

Bill Poster's

Wallpapering A Specialty

SHOW CARDS AND ALL KINDS OF SIGNS

NEON SIGNS

WALL PAPER

PLASTERING

STORE FIXTURES

EXPERT STUCCO WORK

Painting and Decorating

Upholstering

THE WORLD of ART

CHALK TALK

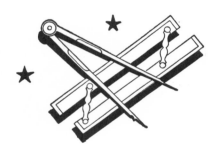

HOME DECORATION DEPARTMENT

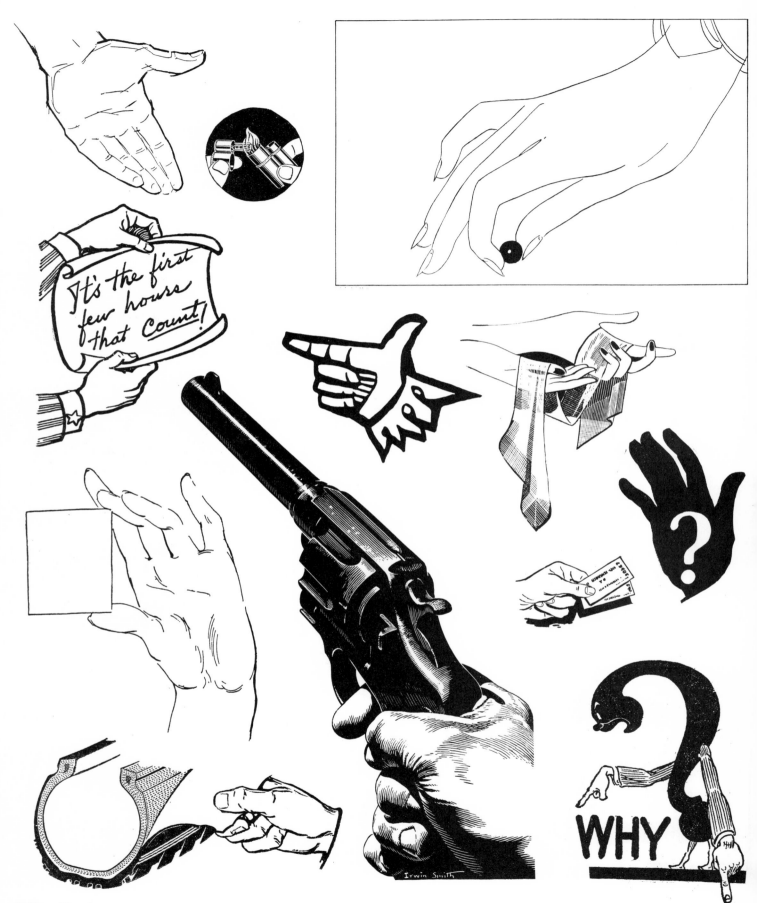

It's the first few hours that Count!

WHY

Irwin Smith

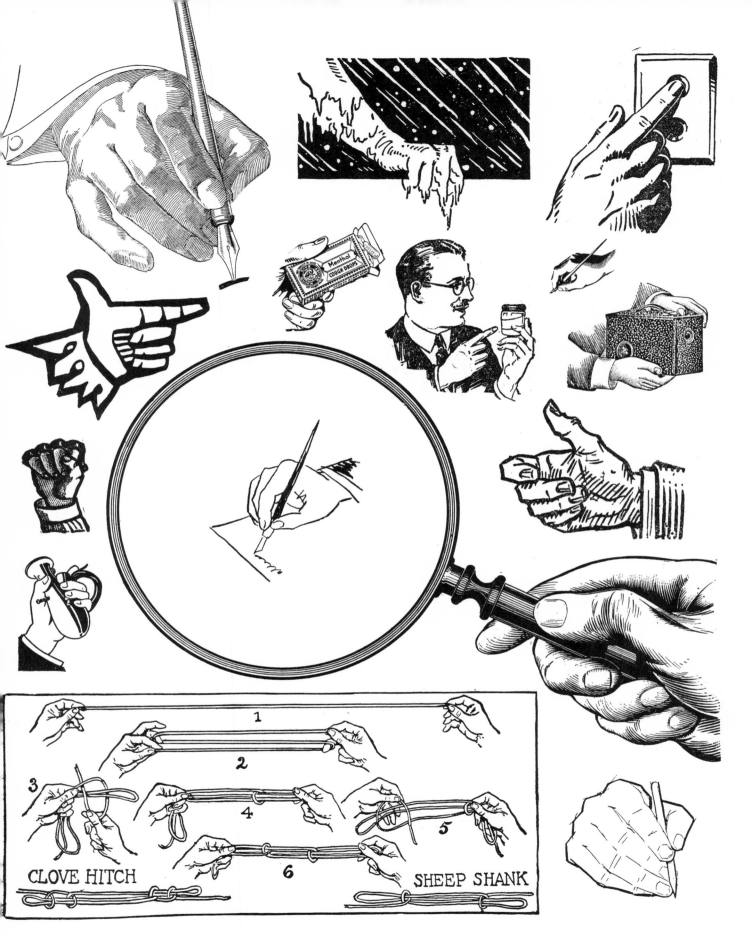

CLOVE HITCH

SHEEP SHANK